MAKEUP

practice face charts

EXTENDED EDITION
200 pages & 10 different faces

This book belongs to the Makeup artist

____

KITTEN SYNDICATE

Try your colors

Notes

Try your colors

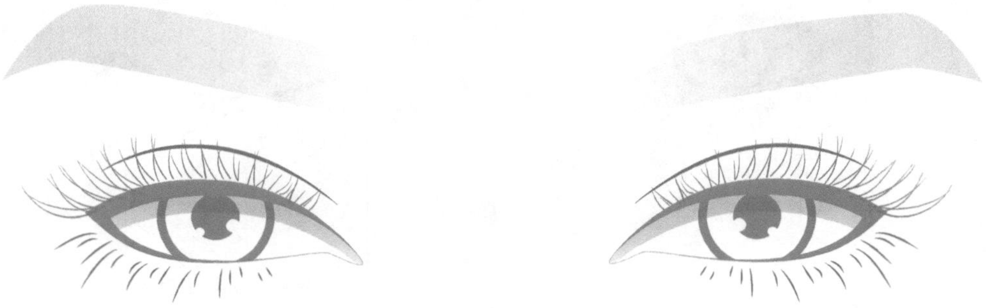

Notes

Try your colors

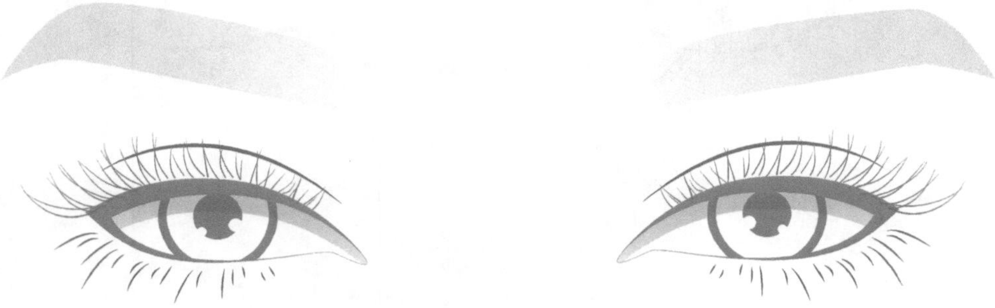

Notes

Try your colors

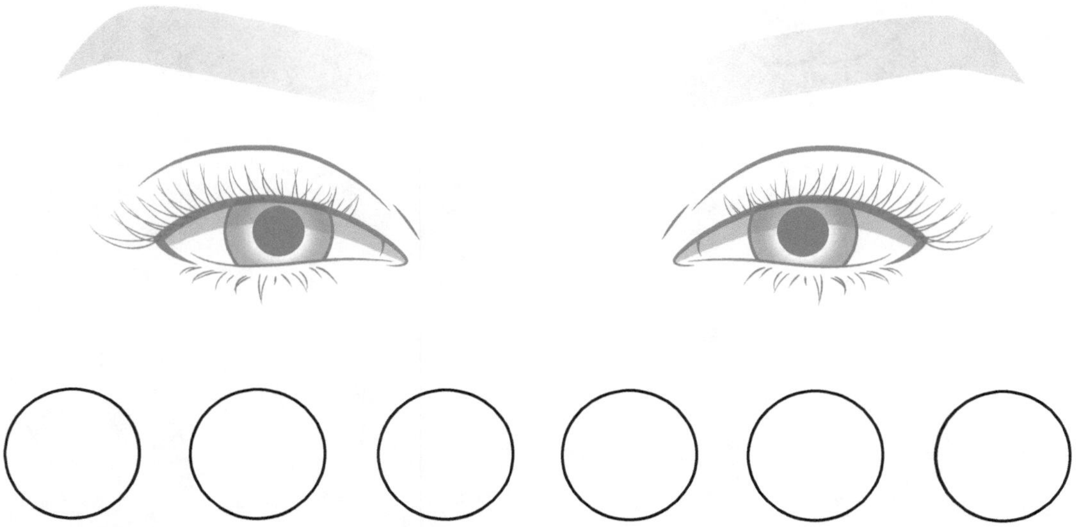

Notes

Try your colors

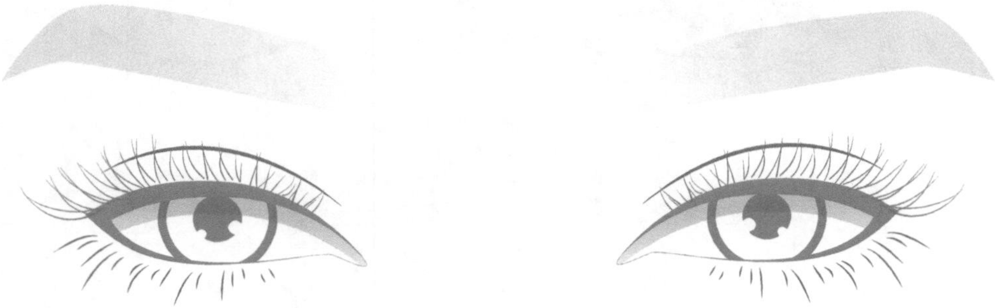

Notes

Try your colors

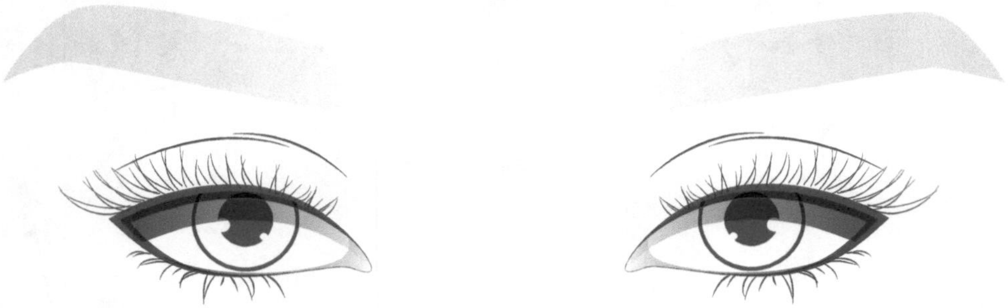

Notes

Try your colors

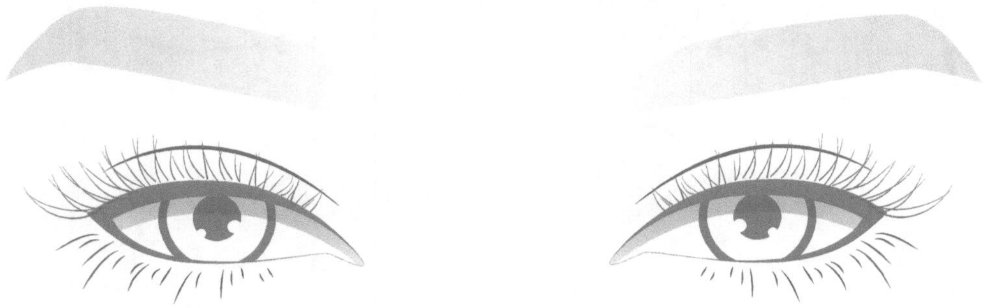

Notes

Try your colors

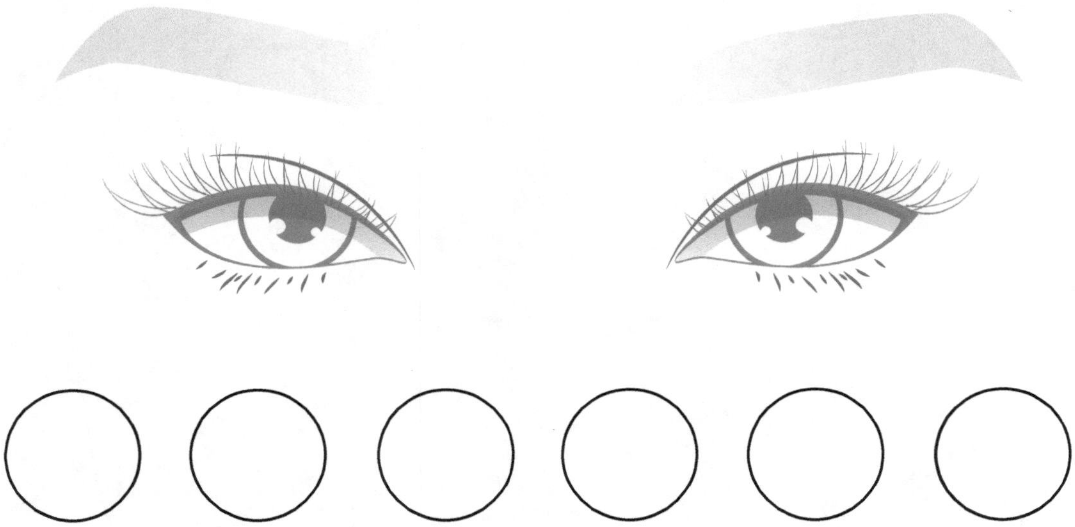

Notes

Try your colors

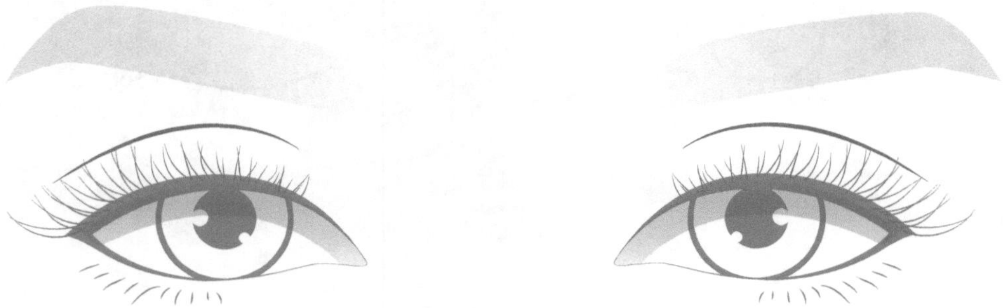

Notes

Try your colors

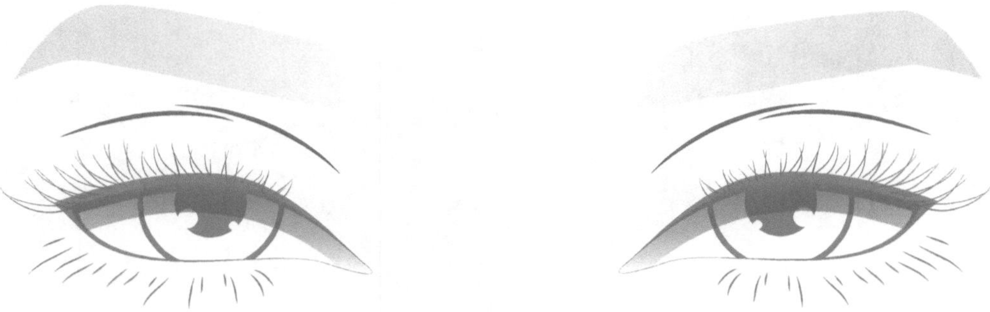

Notes

Try your colors

Notes

Try your colors

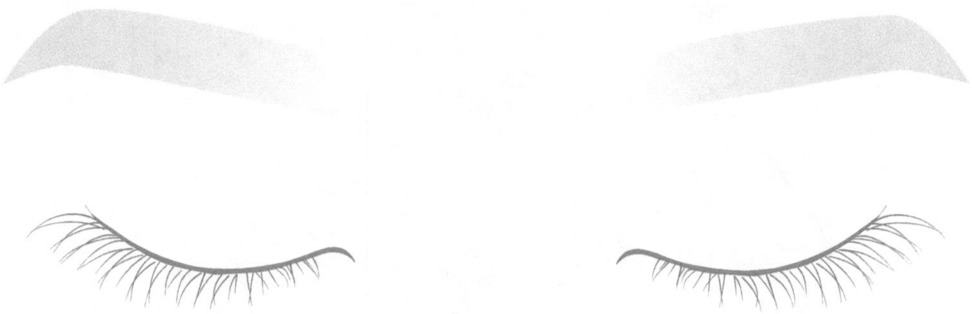

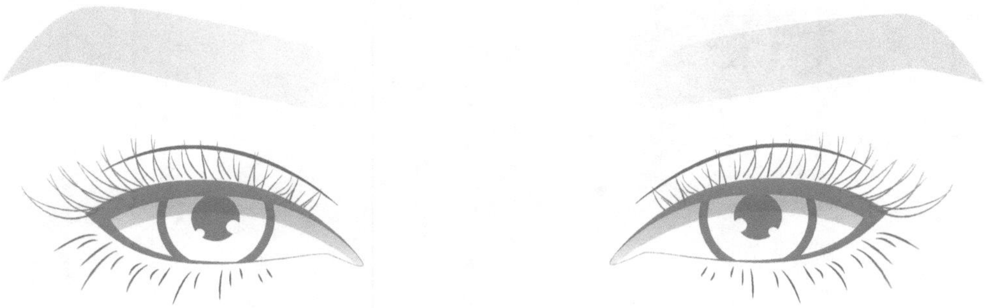

Notes

Try your colors

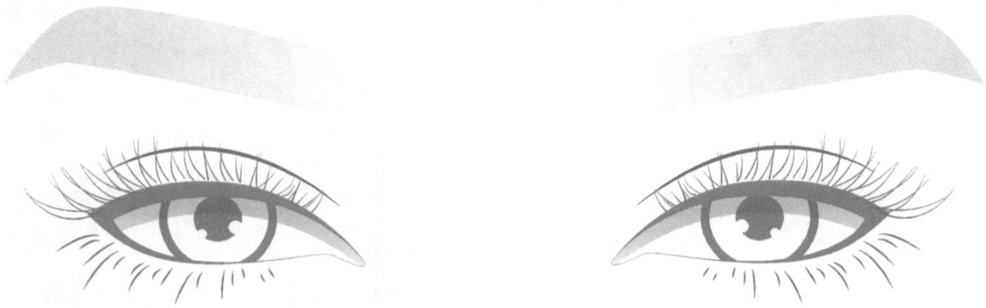

Notes

Try your colors

Notes

Try your colors

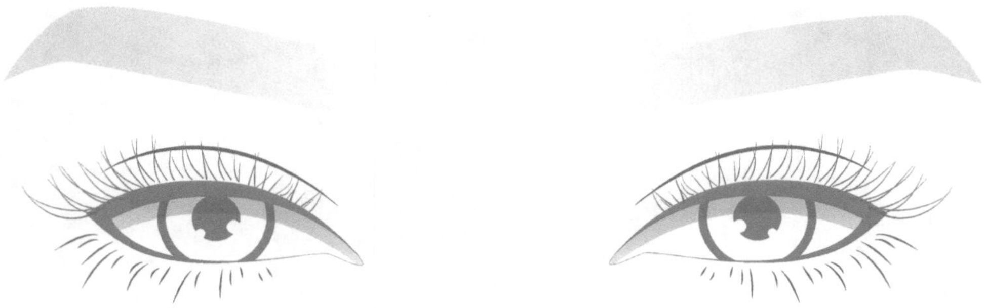

Notes

Try your colors

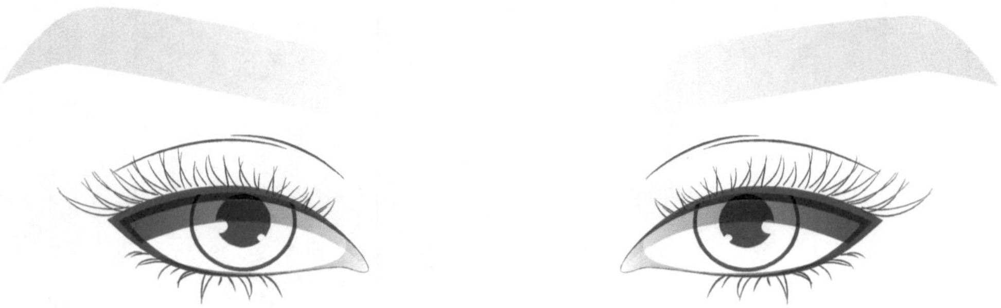

Notes

Try your colors

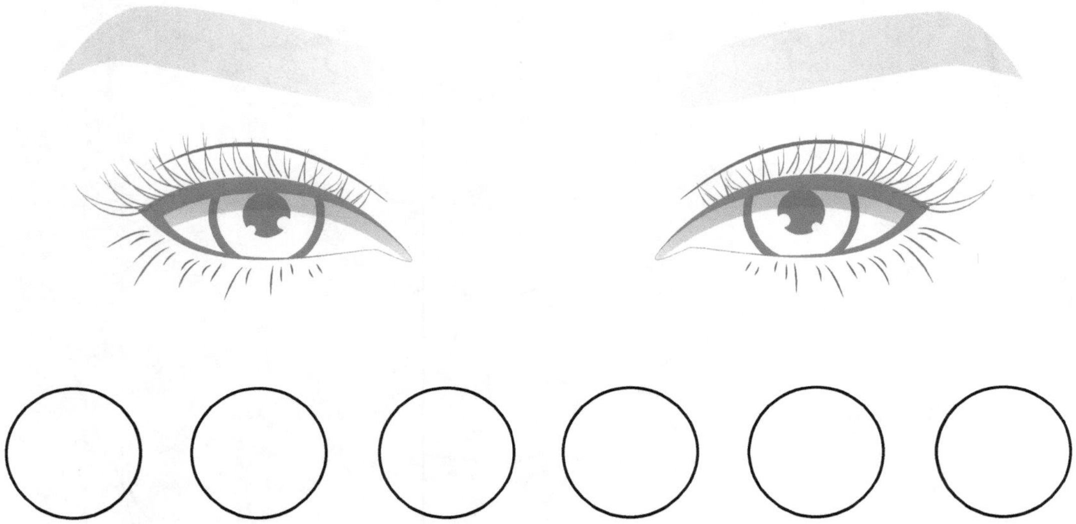

Notes

Try your colors

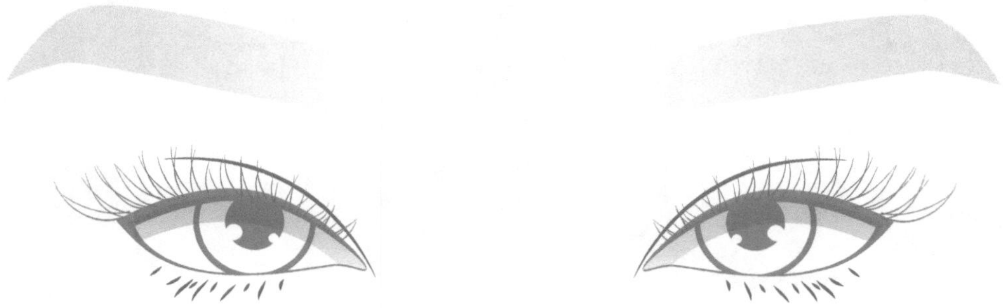

Notes

Try your colors

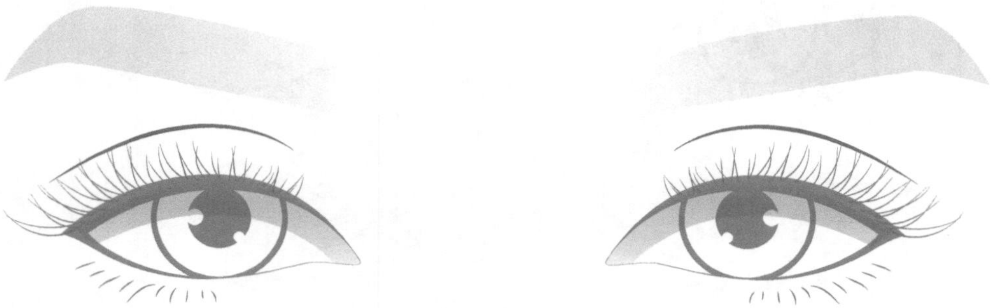

Notes

Try your colors

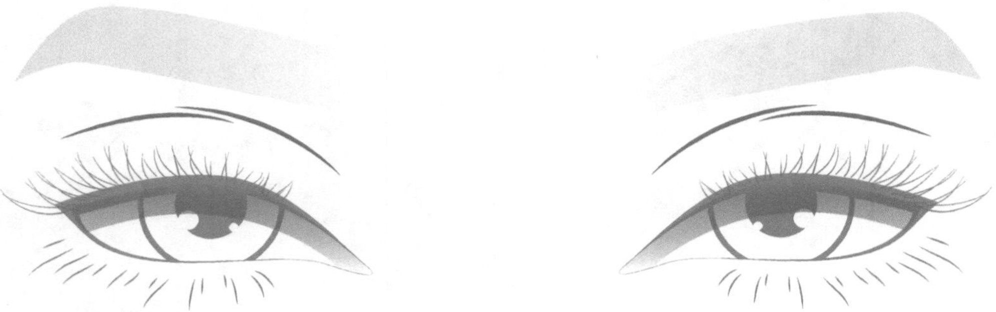

Notes

Try your colors

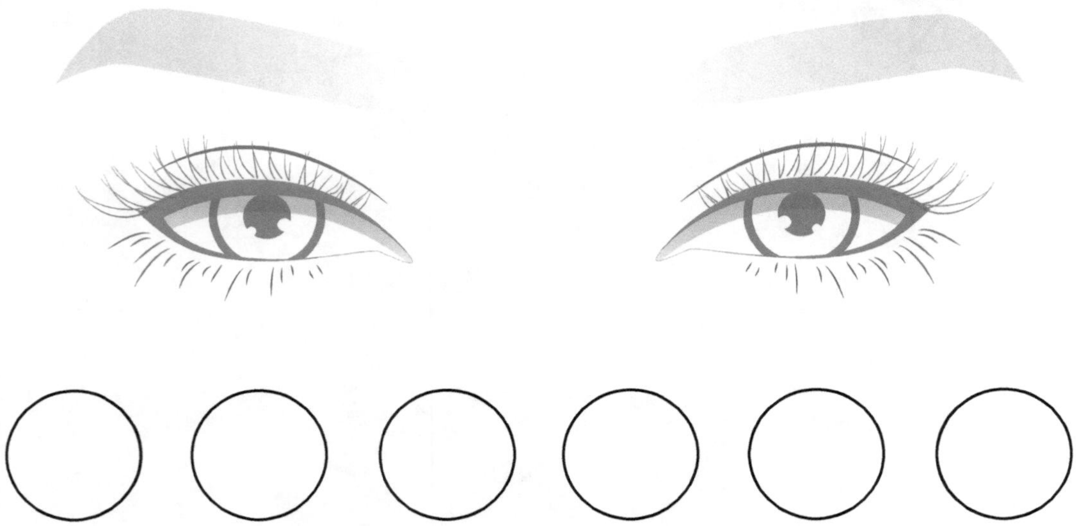

Notes

Try your colors

Notes

Try your colors

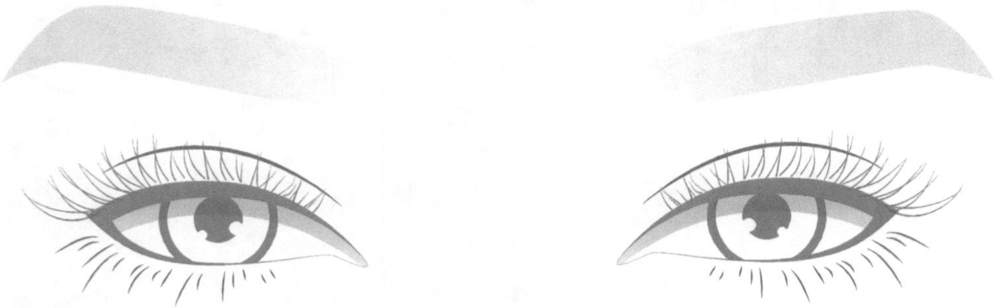

Notes

Try your colors

Notes

Try your colors

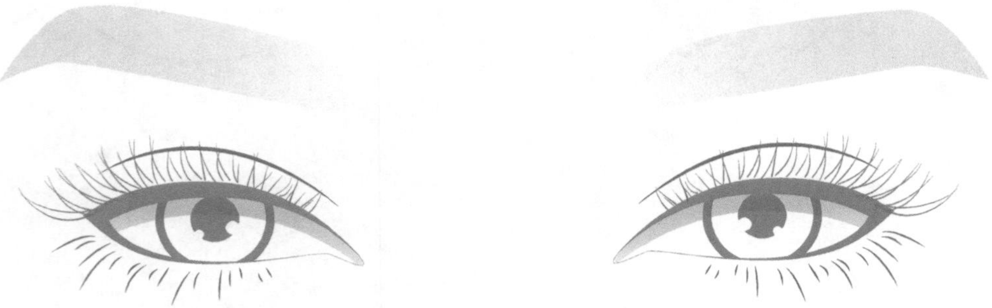

Notes

Try your colors

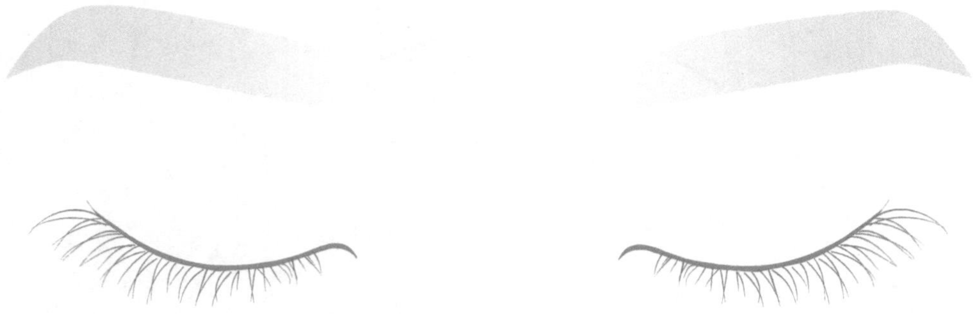

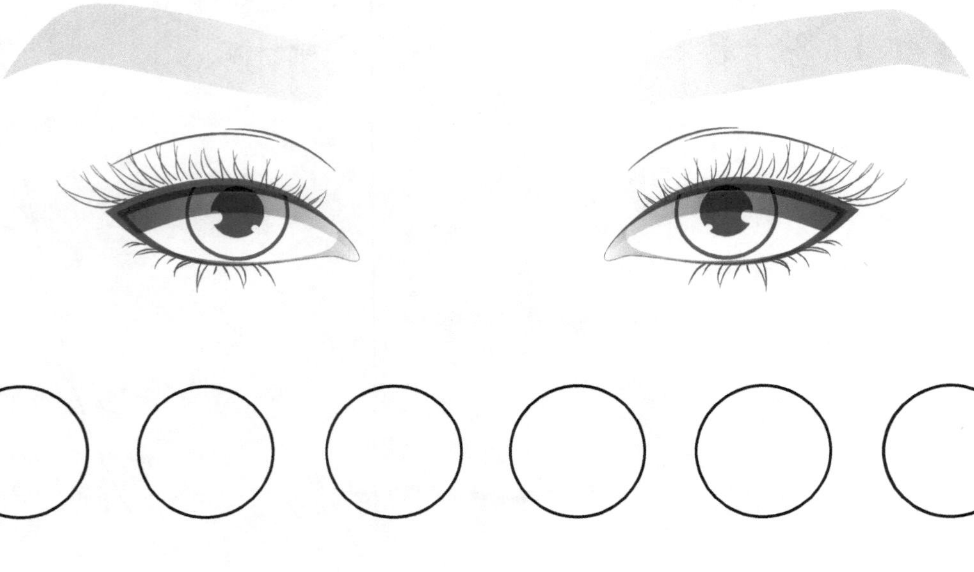

Notes

Try your colors

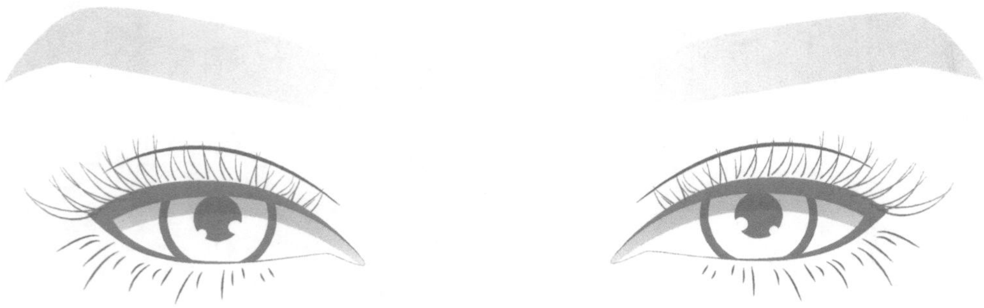

Notes

Try your colors

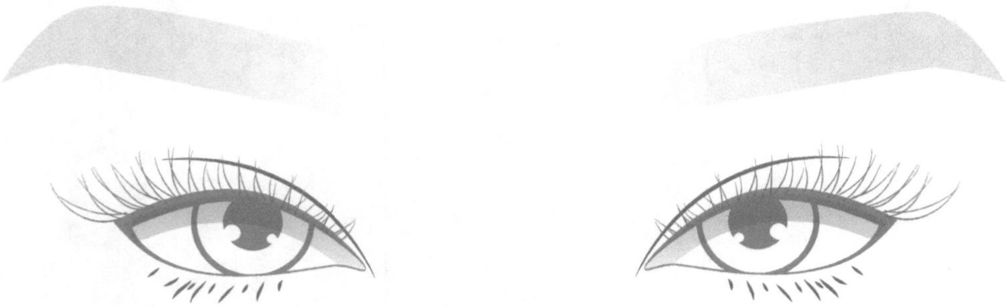

Notes

Try your colors

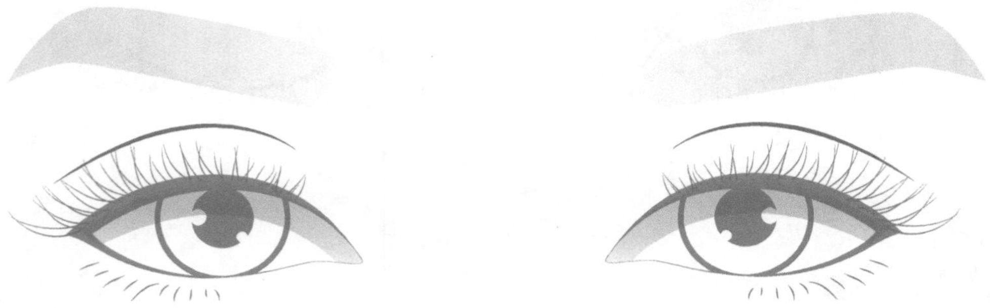

Notes

Try your colors

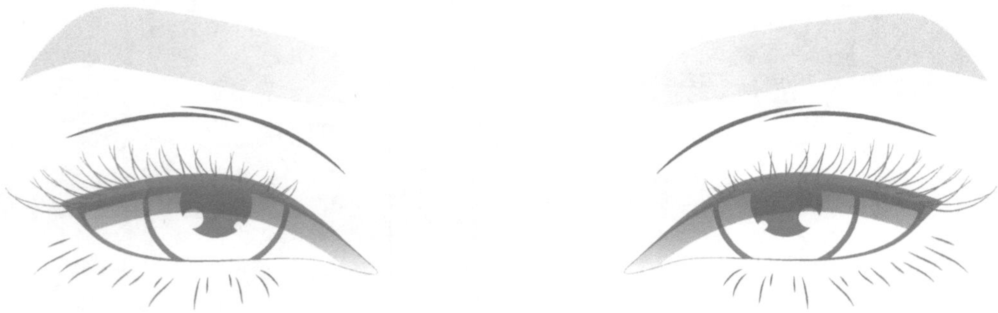

Notes

Try your colors

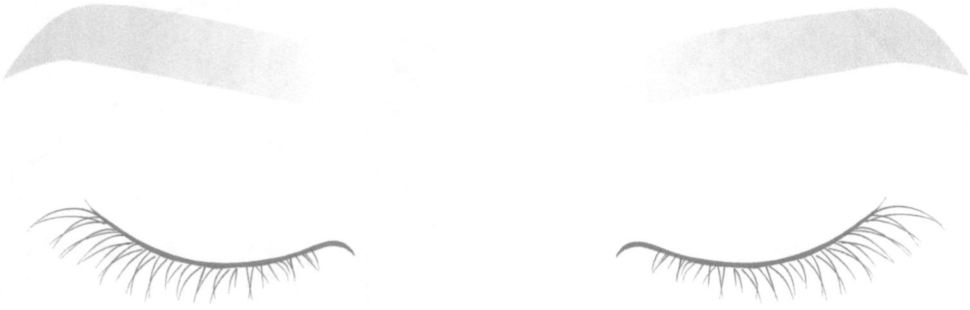

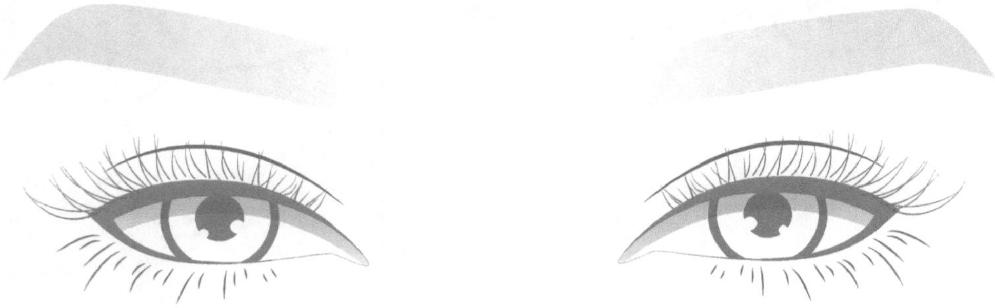

Notes

Try your colors

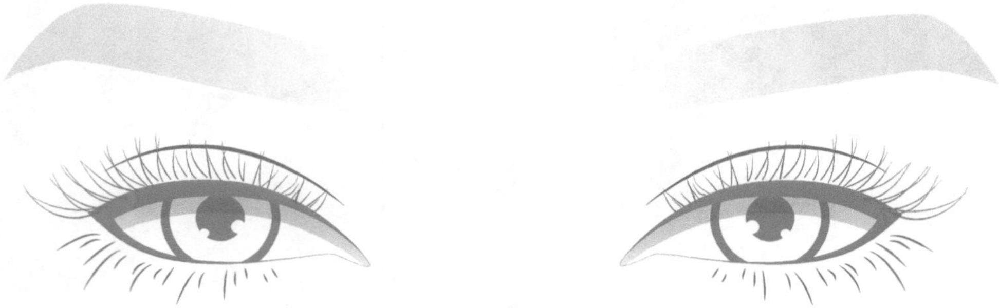

Notes

Try your colors

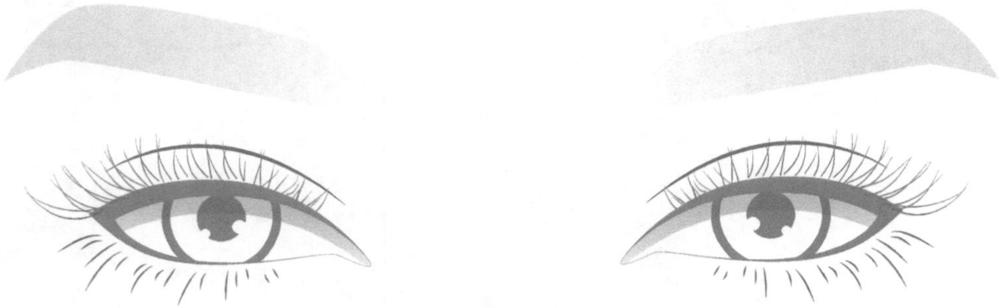

Notes

Try your colors

Notes

Try your colors

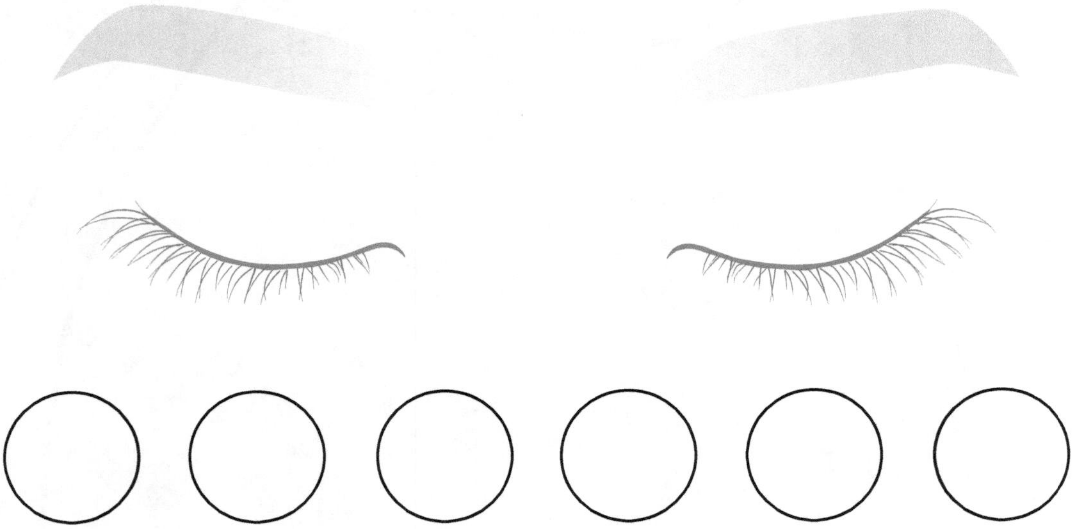

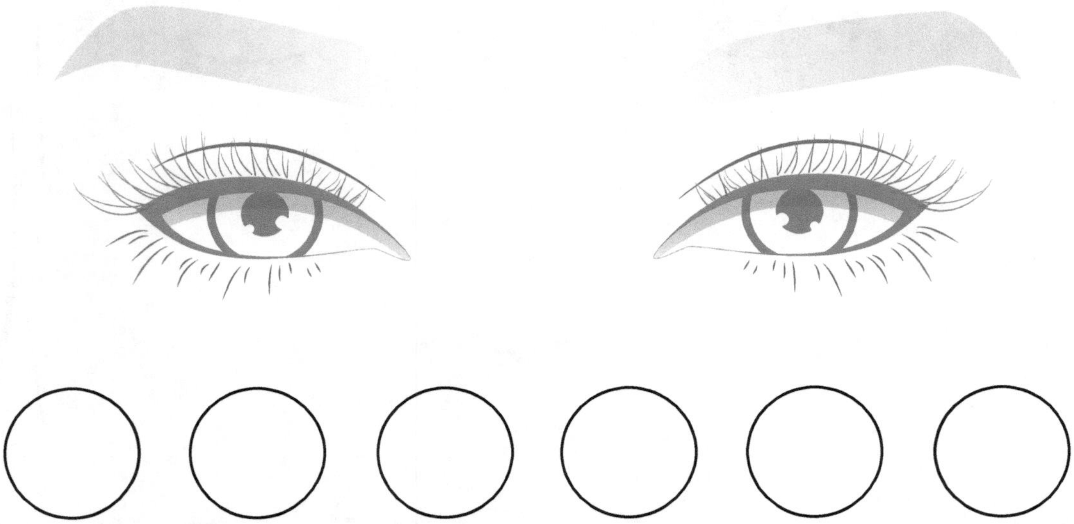

Notes

Try your colors

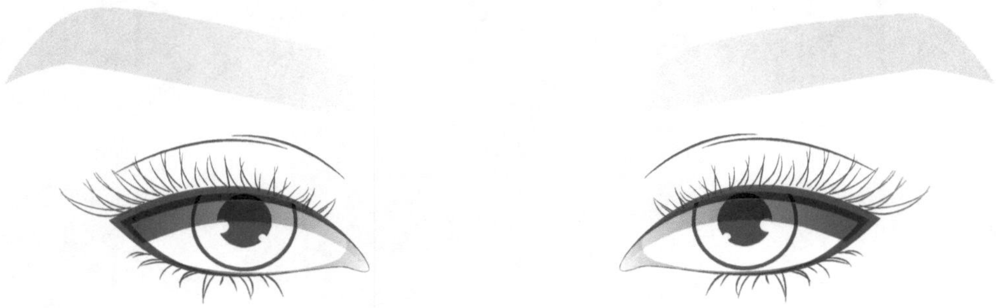

Notes

Try your colors

Notes

Try your colors

Notes

Try your colors

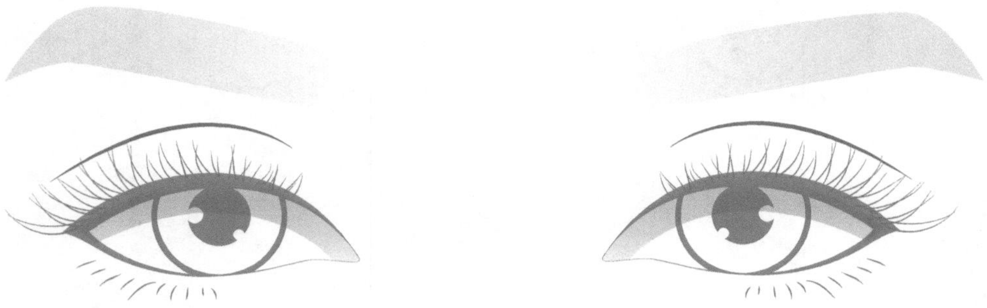

Notes

Try your colors

Notes

Try your colors

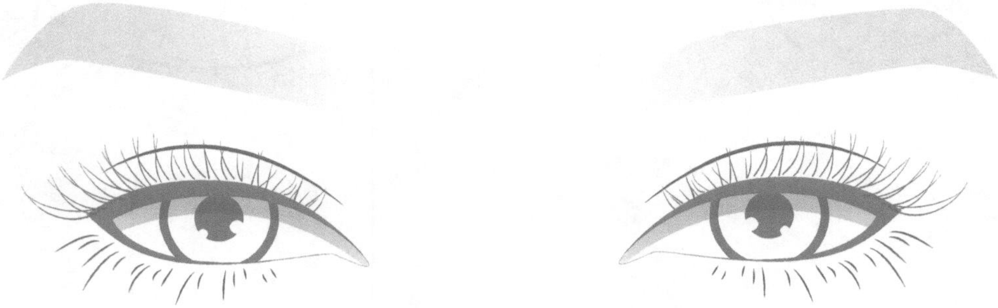

Notes

Try your colors

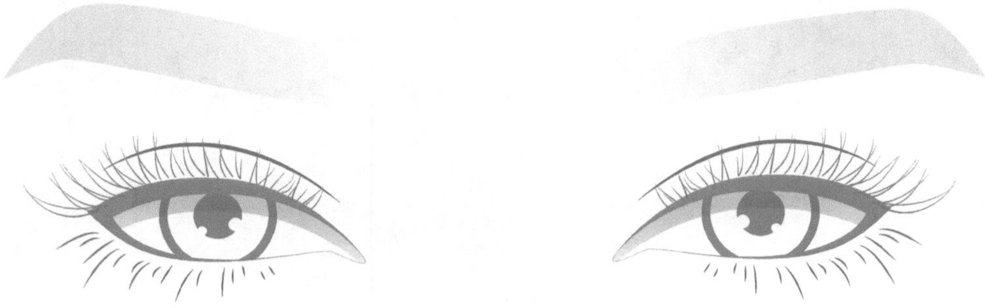

Notes

Try your colors

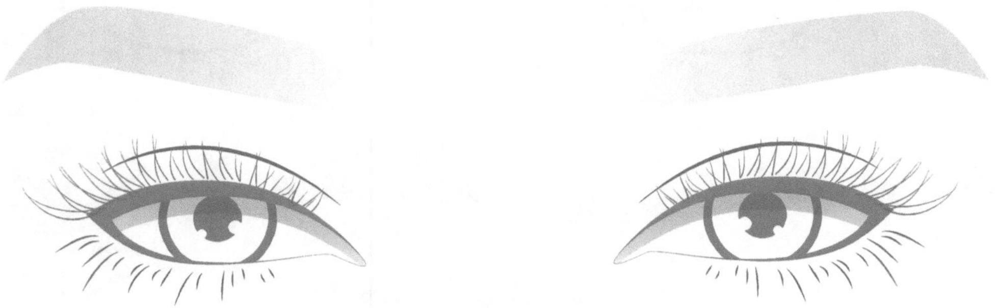

Notes

Try your colors

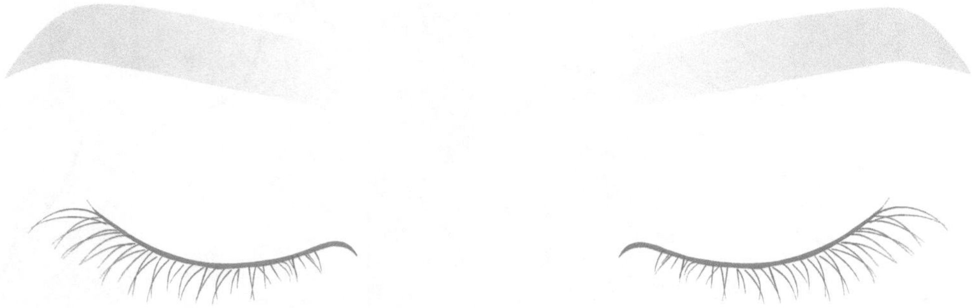

Notes

Try your colors

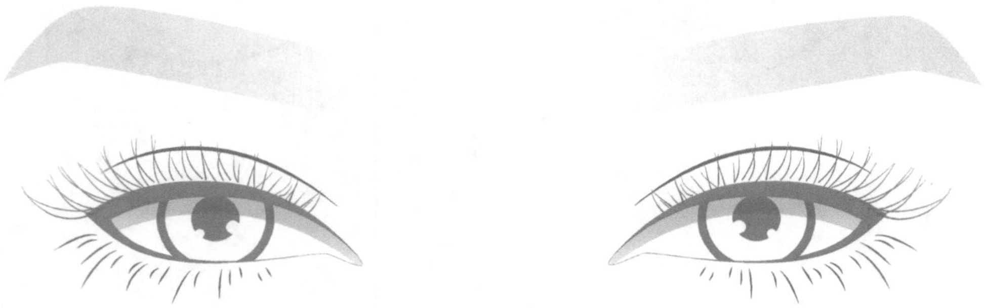

Notes

Try your colors

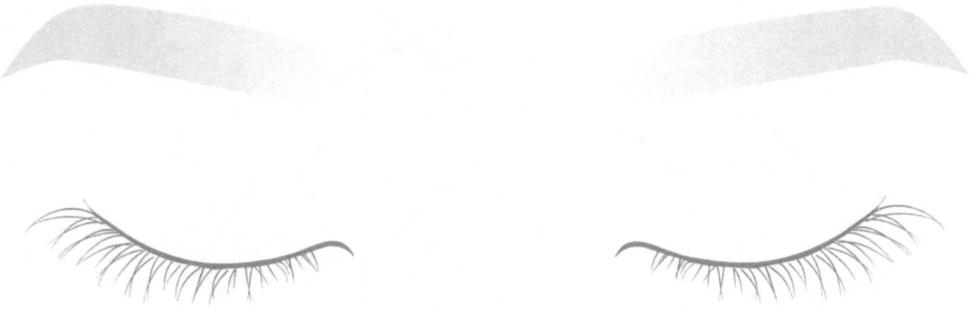

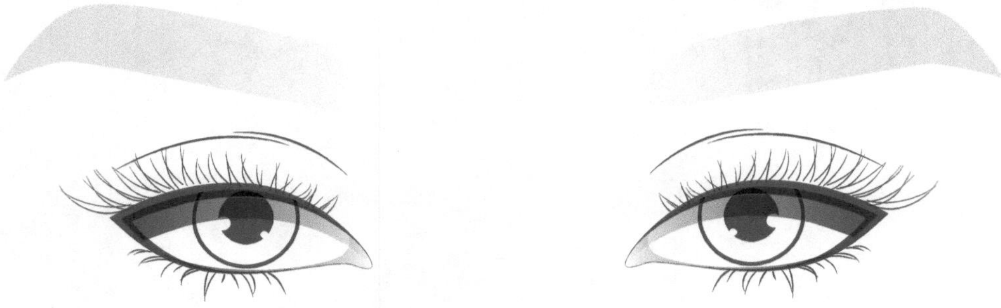

Notes

Try your colors

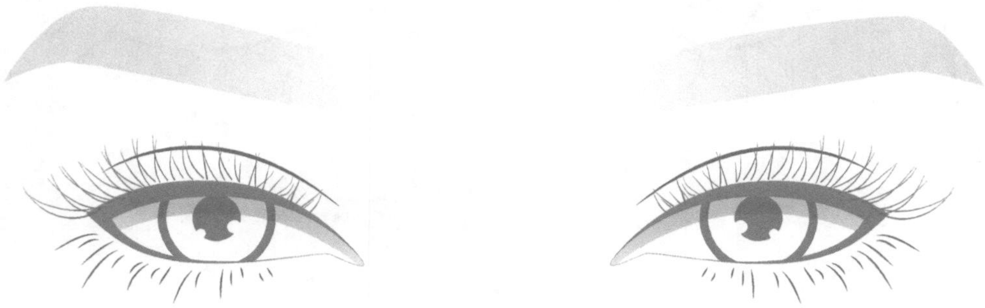

Notes

Try your colors

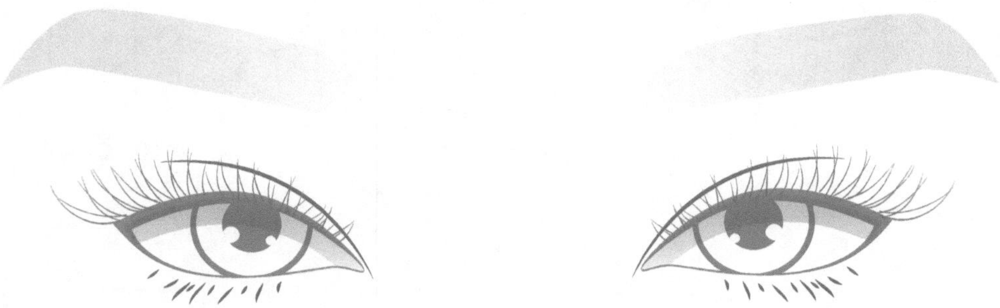

Notes

Try your colors

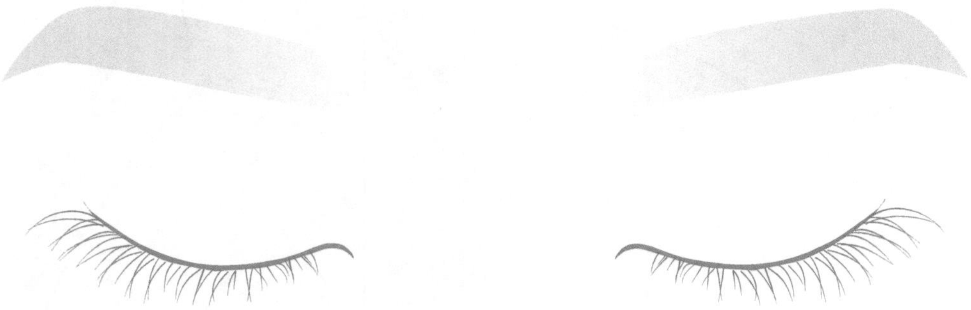

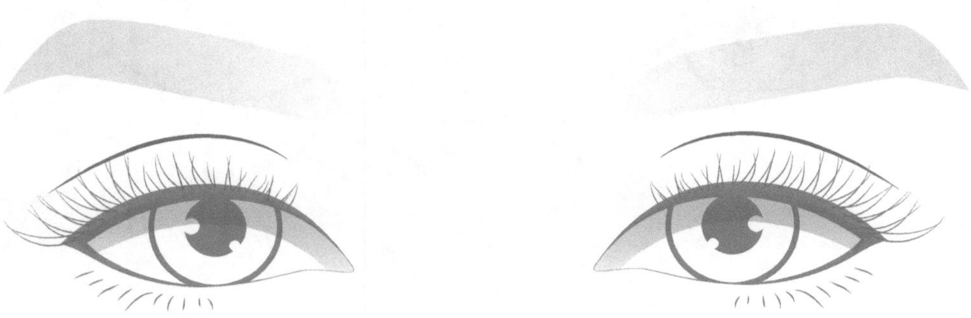

Notes

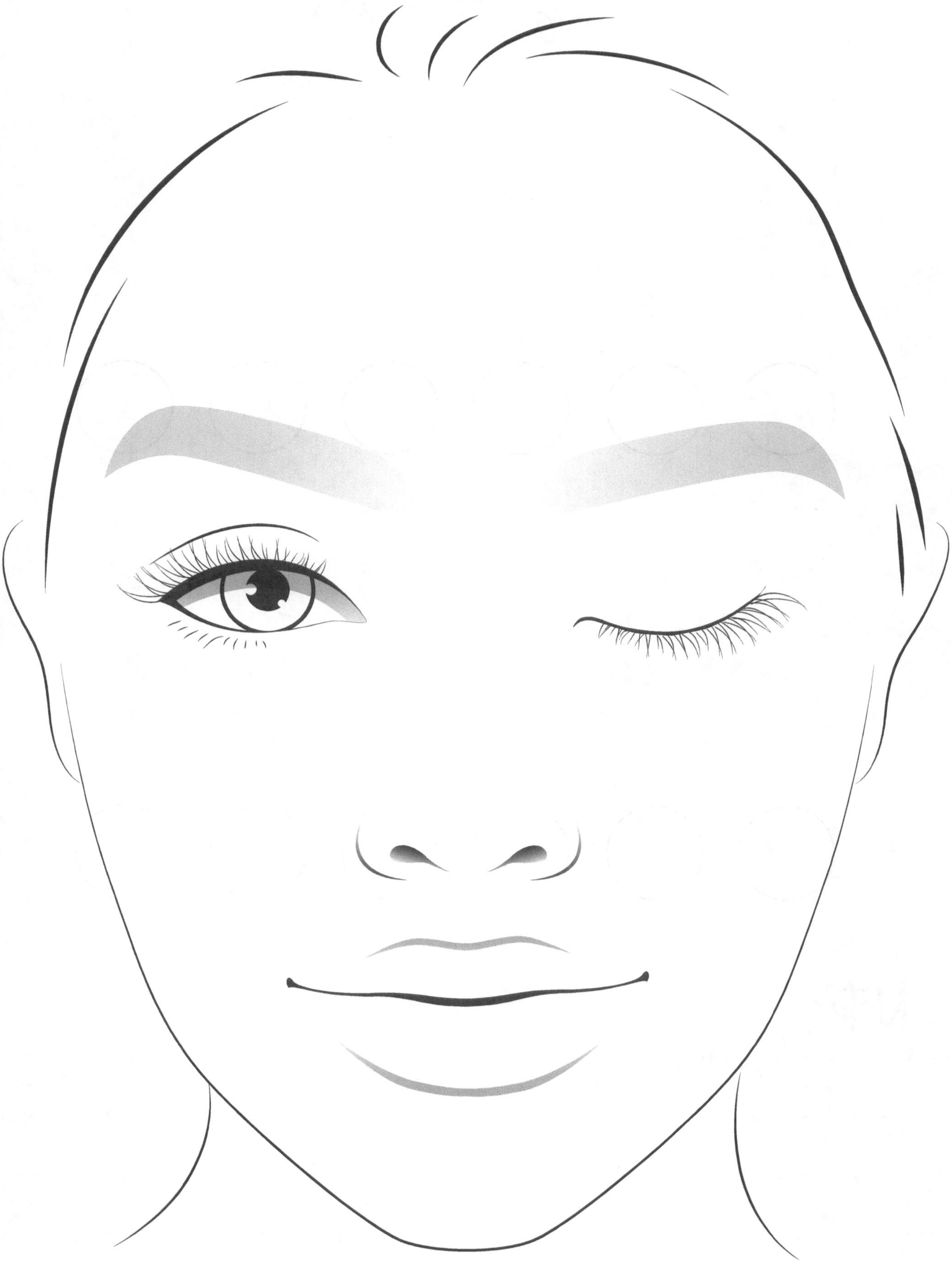

Try your colors

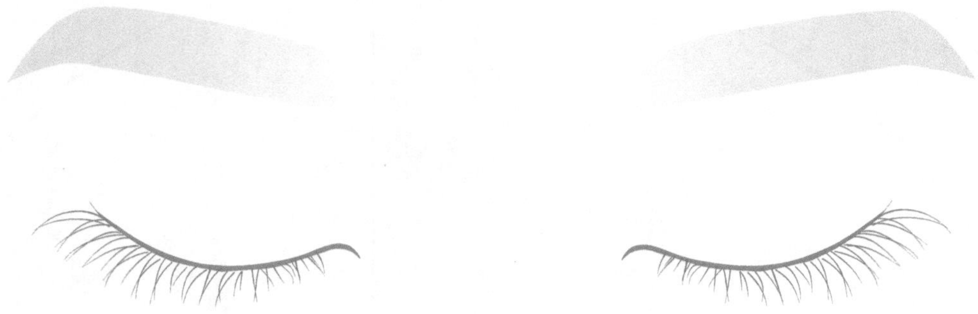

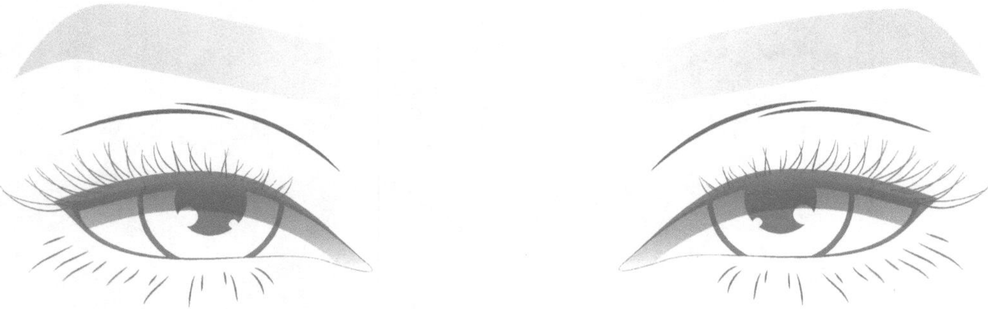

Notes

Try your colors

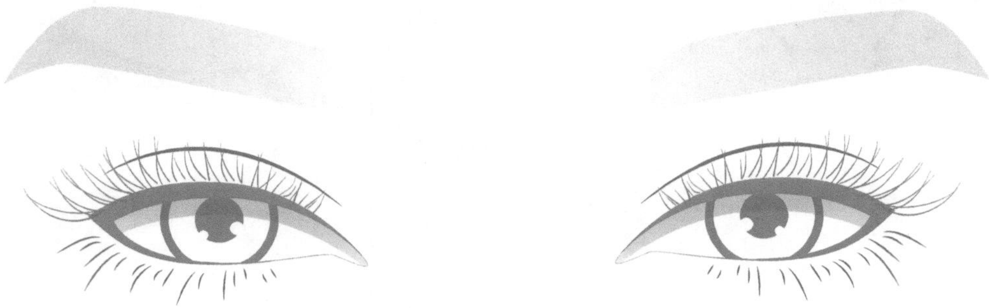

Notes

Try your colors

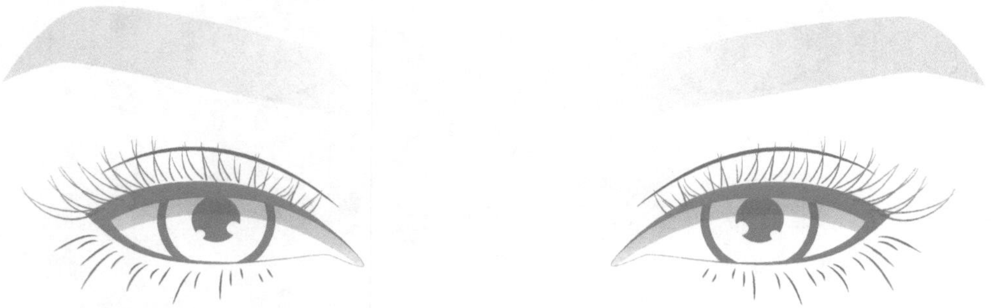

Notes

Try your colors

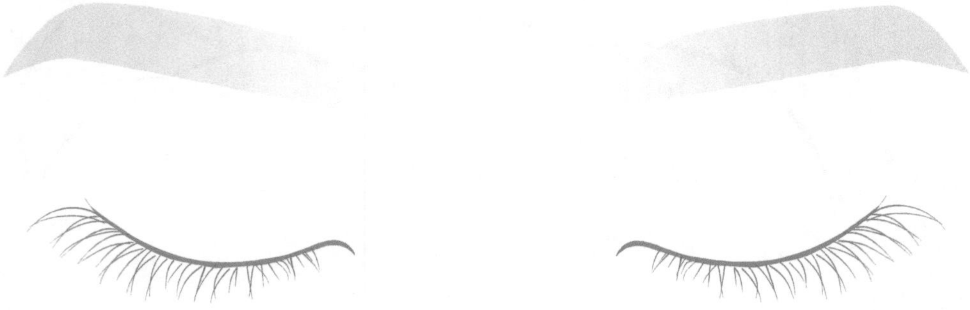

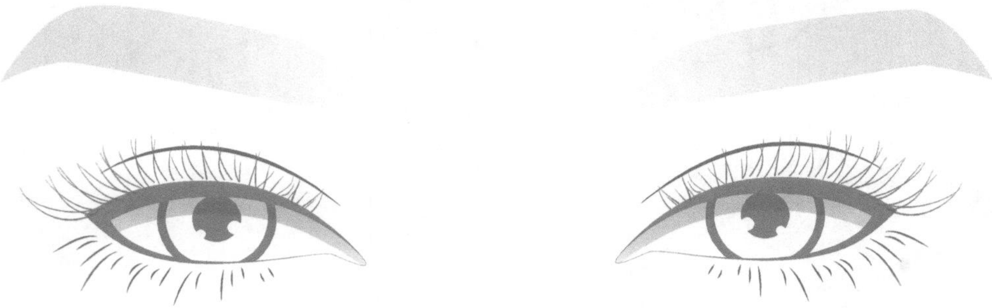

Notes

Try your colors

Notes

Try your colors

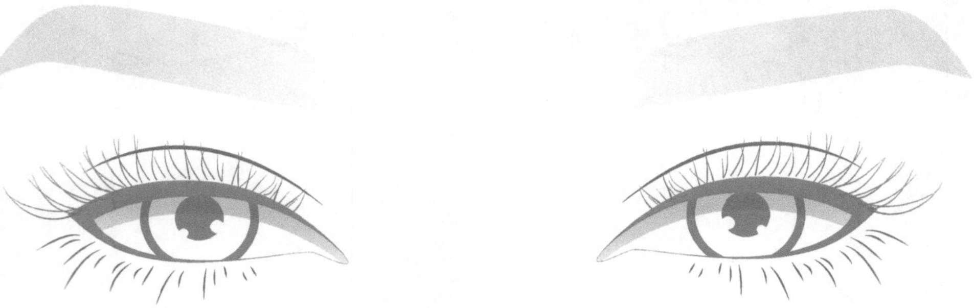

Notes

Try your colors

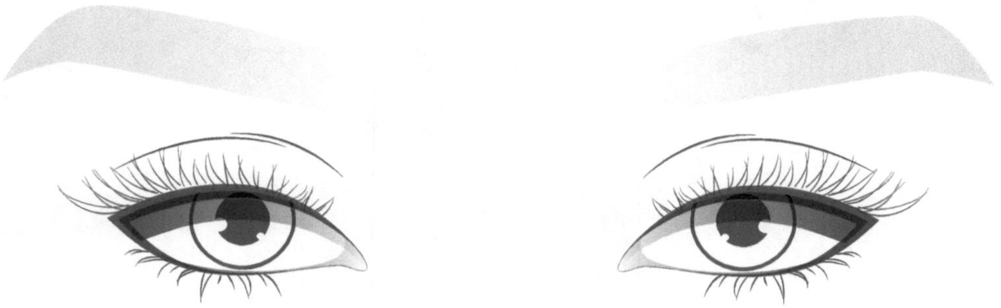

Notes

Try your colors

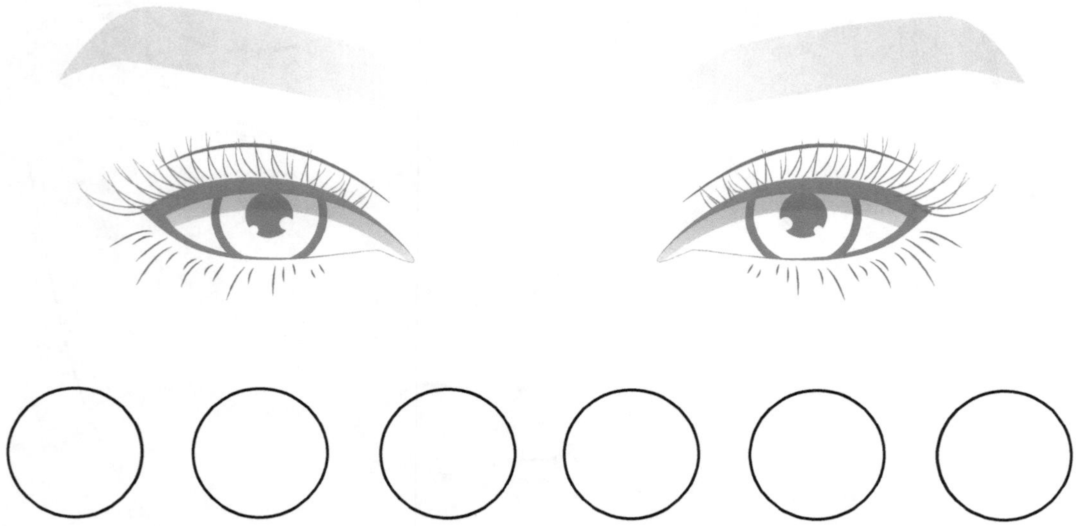

Notes

Try your colors

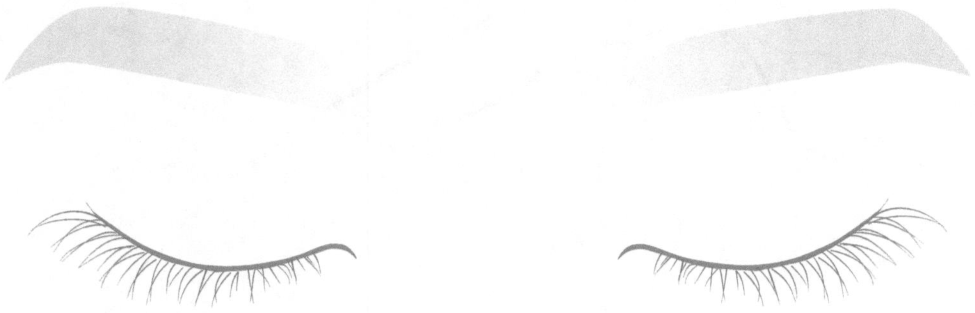

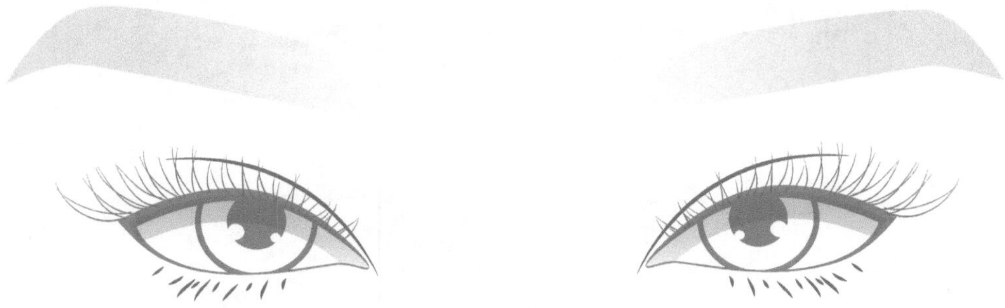

Notes

Try your colors

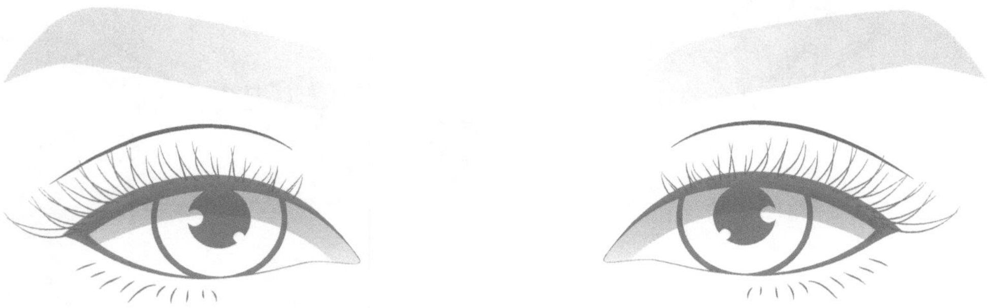

Notes

Try your colors

Notes

Try your colors

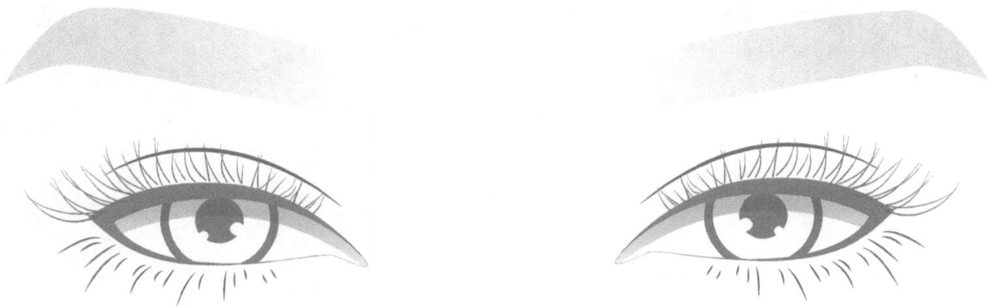

Notes

Try your colors

Notes

Try your colors

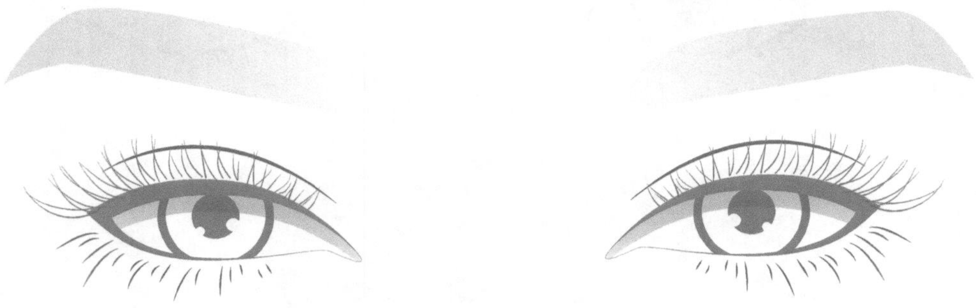

Notes

Try your colors

Notes

Try your colors

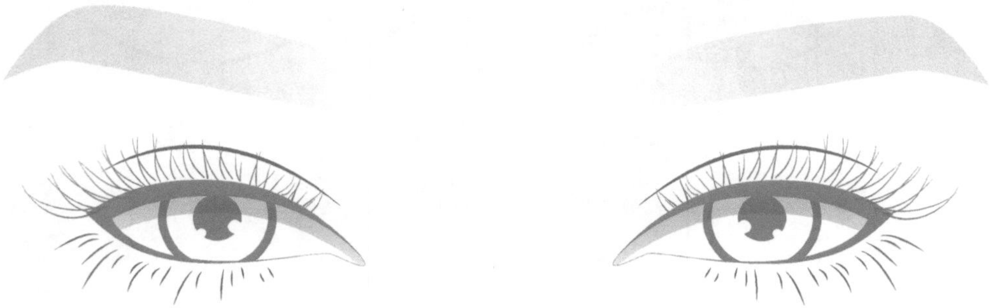

Notes

Try your colors

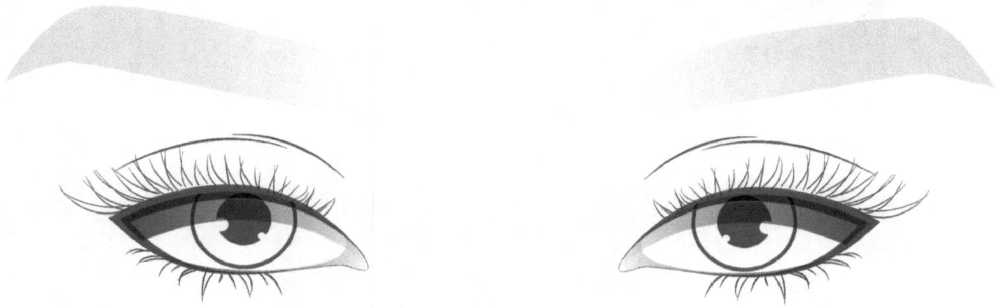

Notes

Try your colors

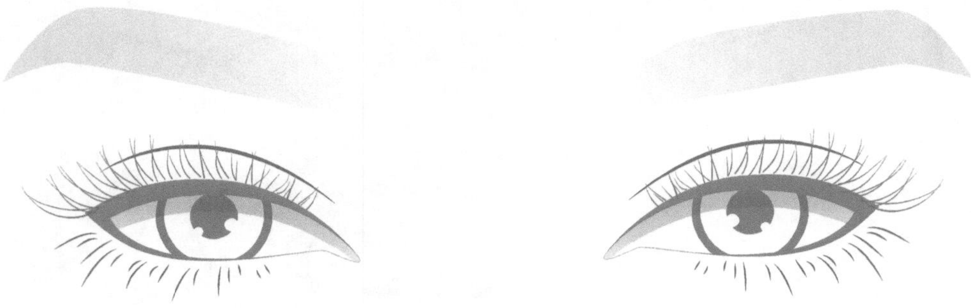

Notes

Try your colors

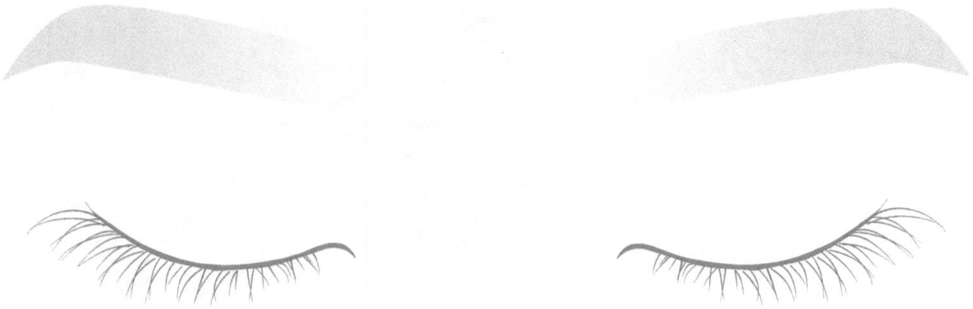

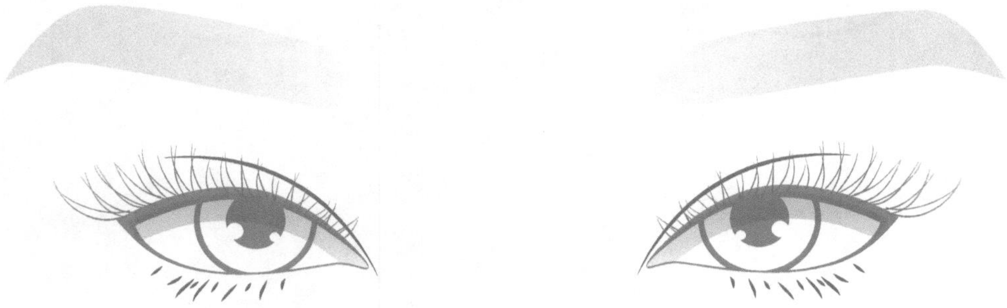

Notes

Try your colors

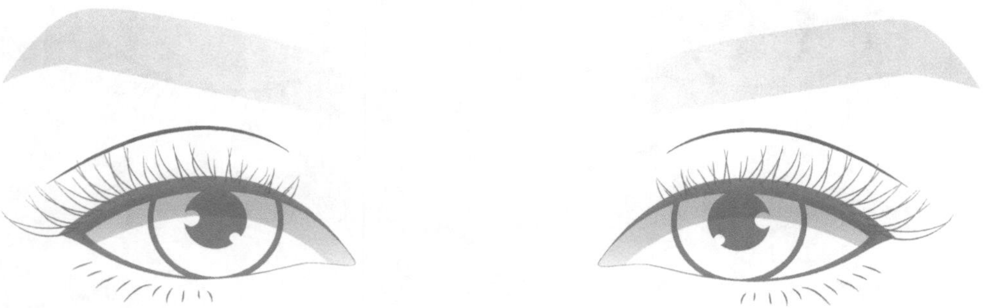

Notes

Try your colors

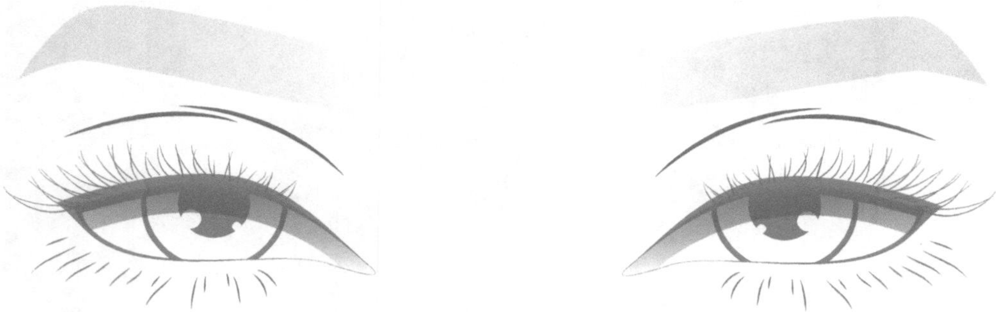

Notes

Try your colors

Notes

Try your colors

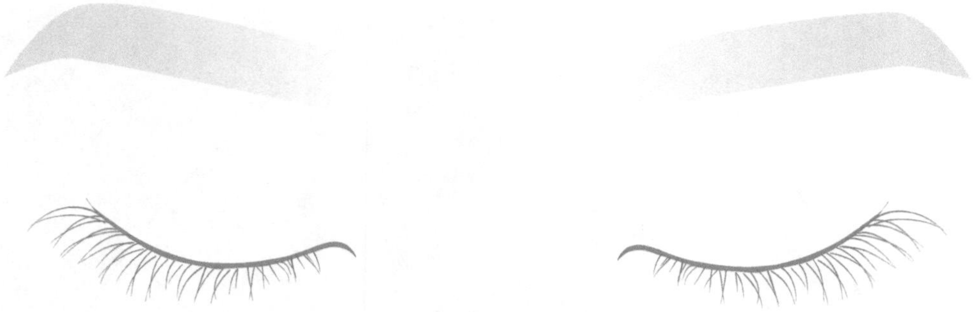

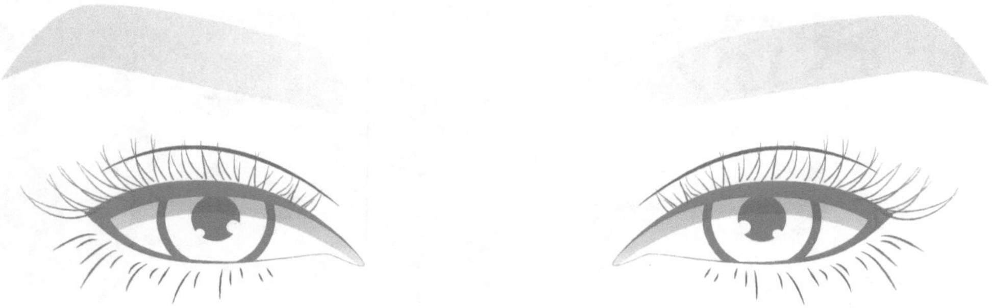

Notes

Try your colors

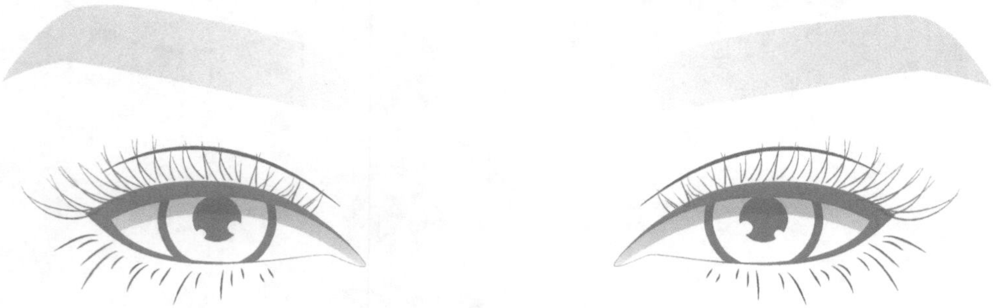

Notes

Try your colors

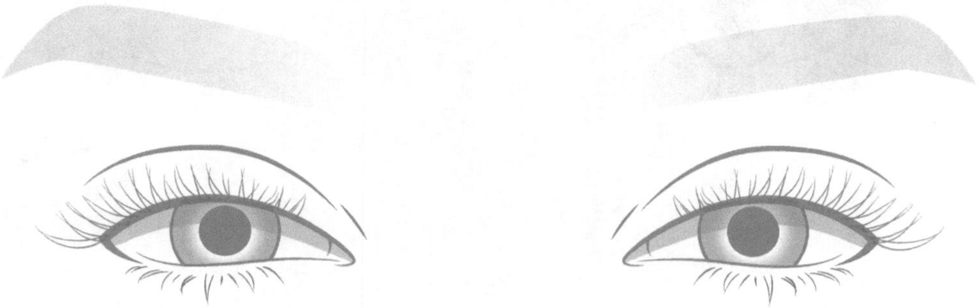

Notes

Try your colors

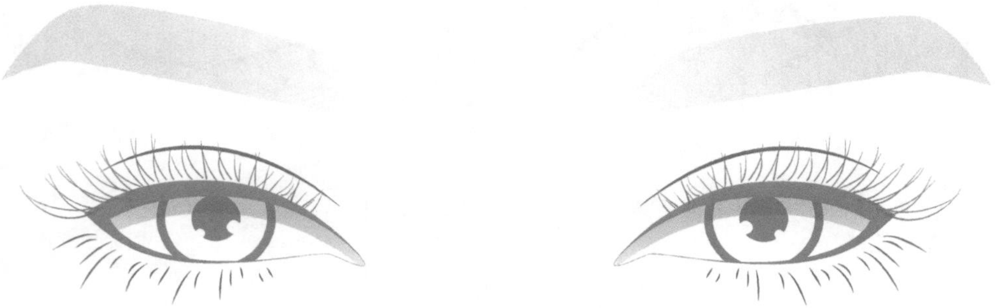

Notes

Try your colors

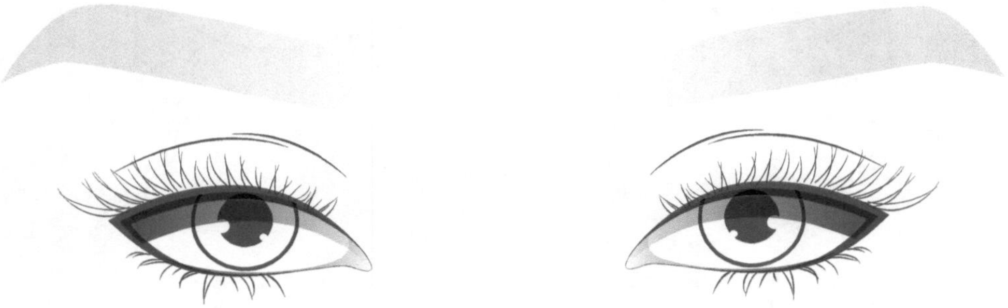

Notes

Try your colors

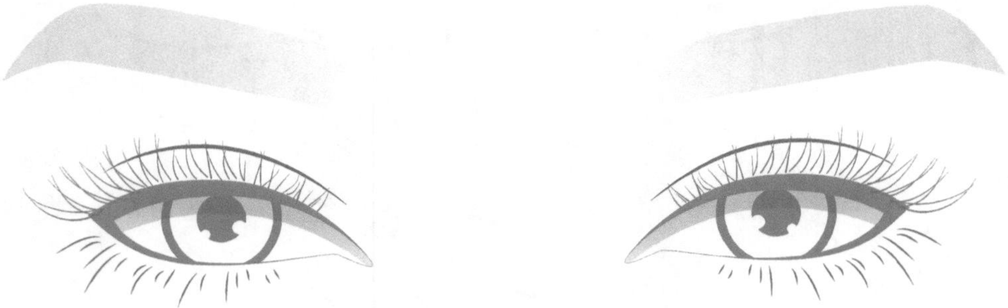

Notes

Try your colors

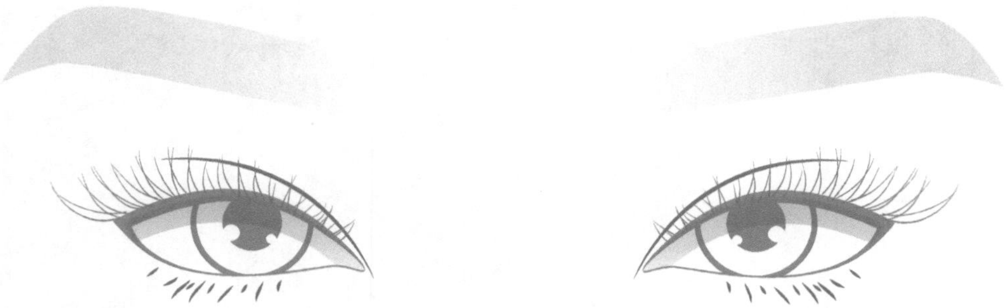

Notes

Try your colors

Notes

Try your colors

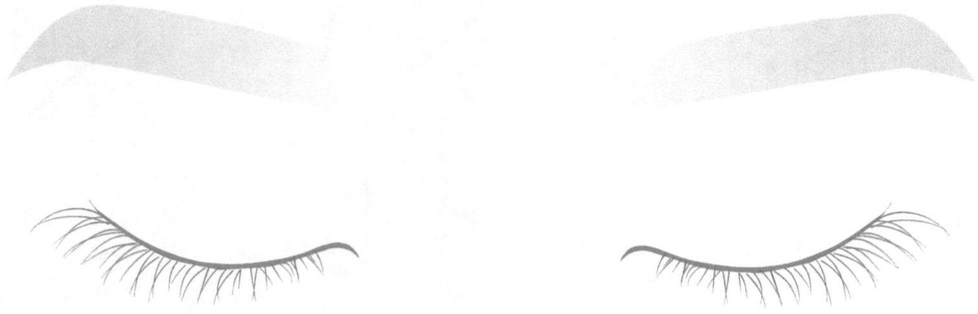

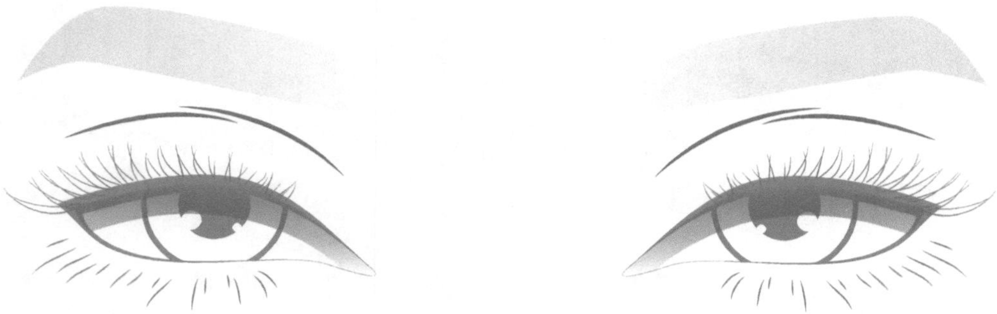

Notes

Try your colors

Notes

Try your colors

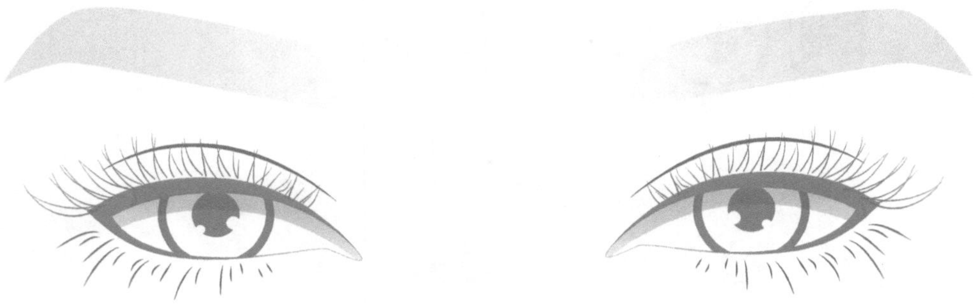

Notes

Try your colors

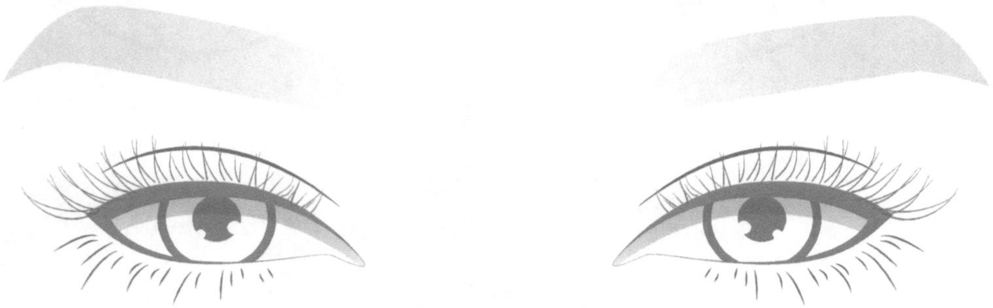

Notes

Try your colors

Notes

Try your colors

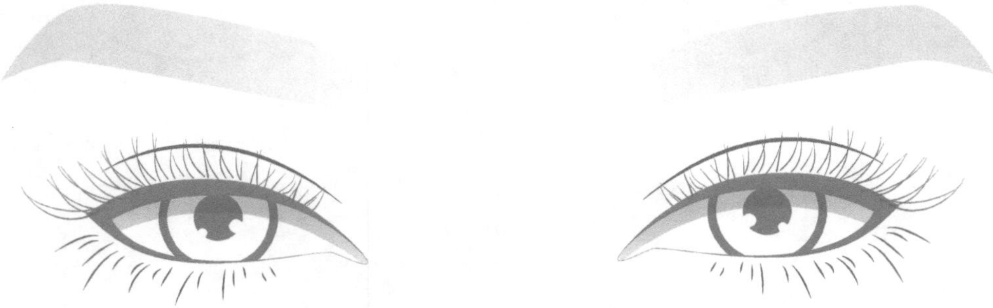

Notes

Try your colors

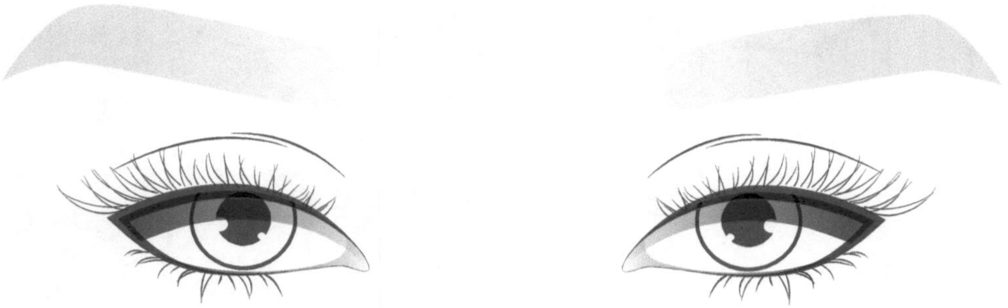

Notes

Try your colors

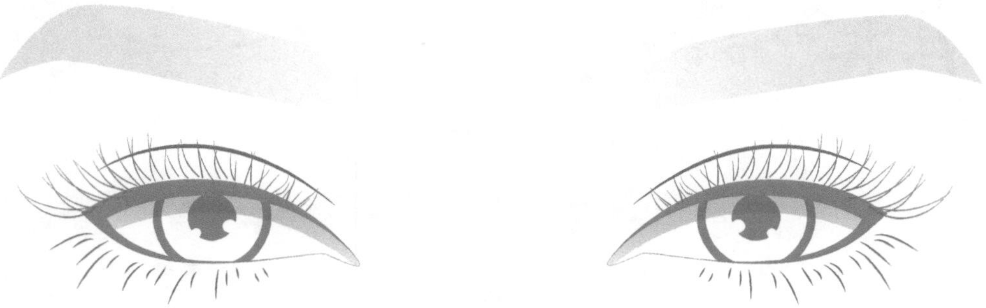

Notes

Try your colors

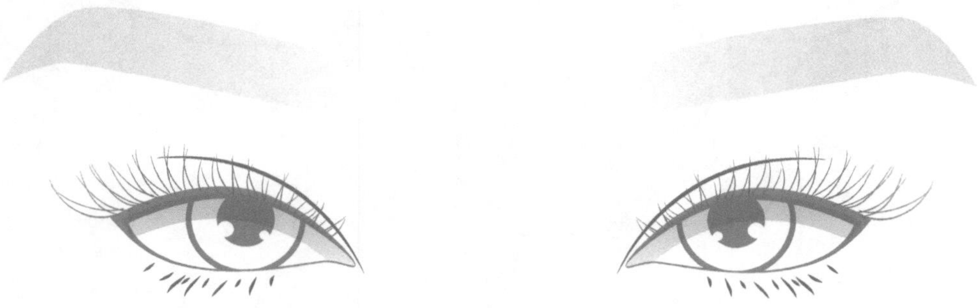

Notes

Try your colors

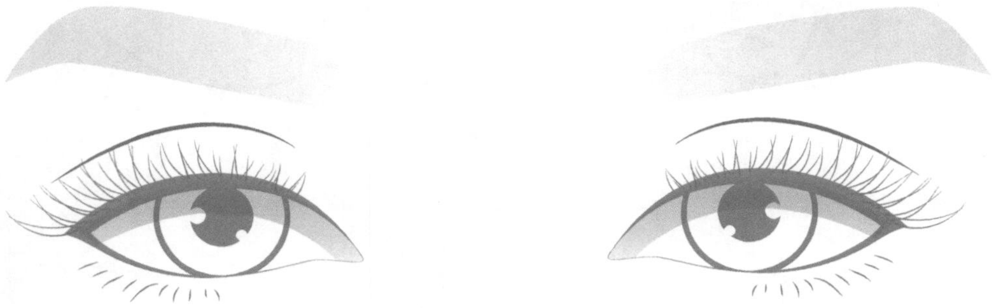

Notes

Try your colors

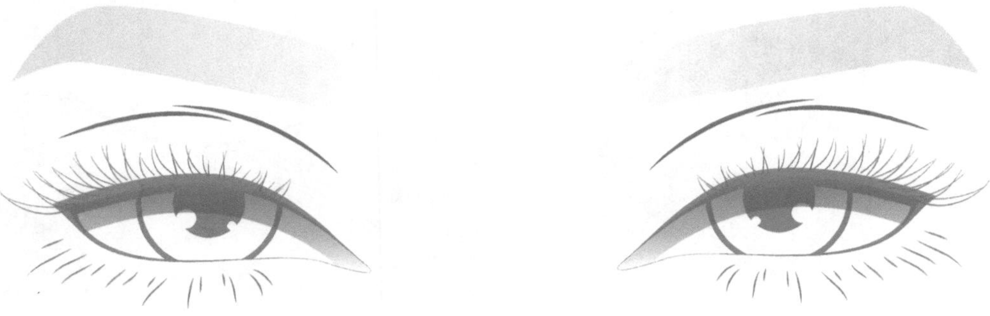

Notes

Try your colors

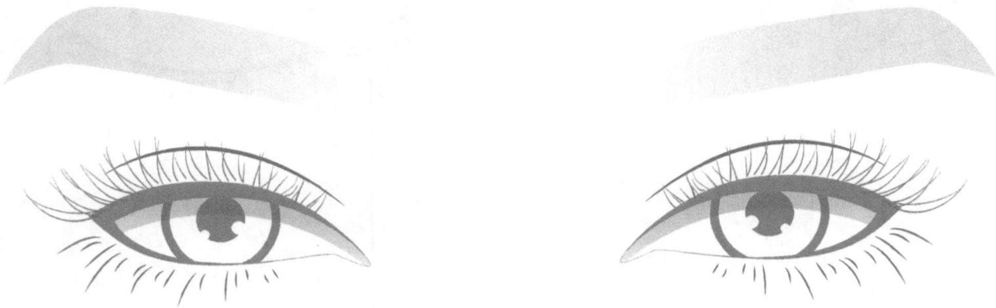

Notes

Try your colors

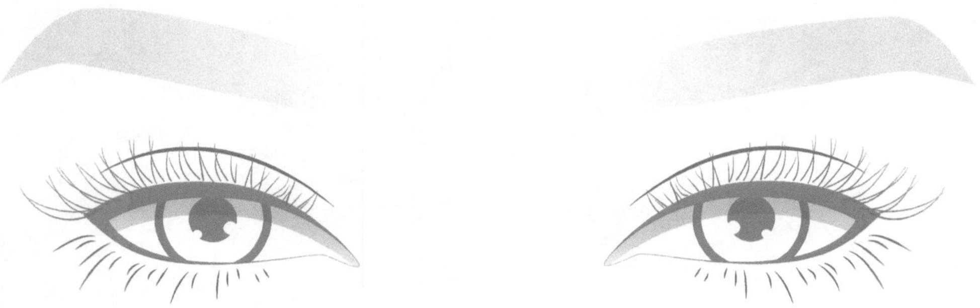

Notes

Try your colors

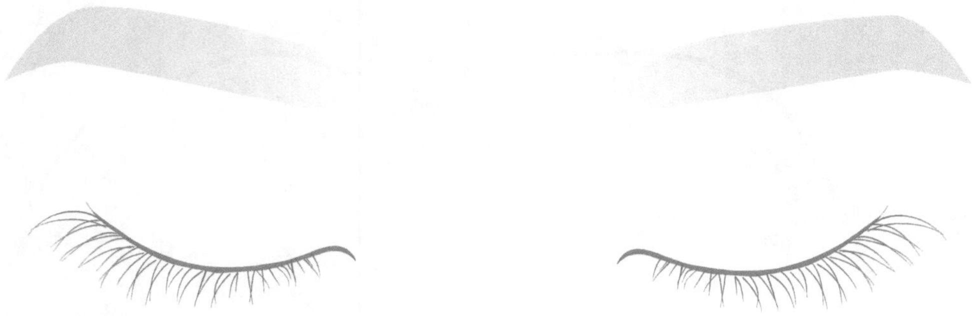

Notes

Try your colors

Notes

Try your colors

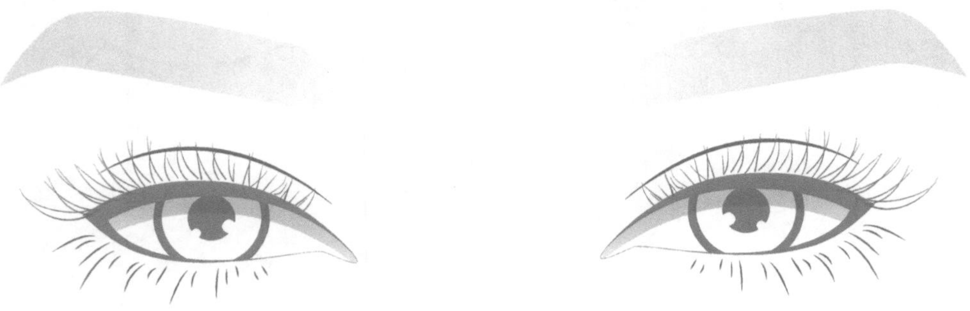

Notes

Try your colors

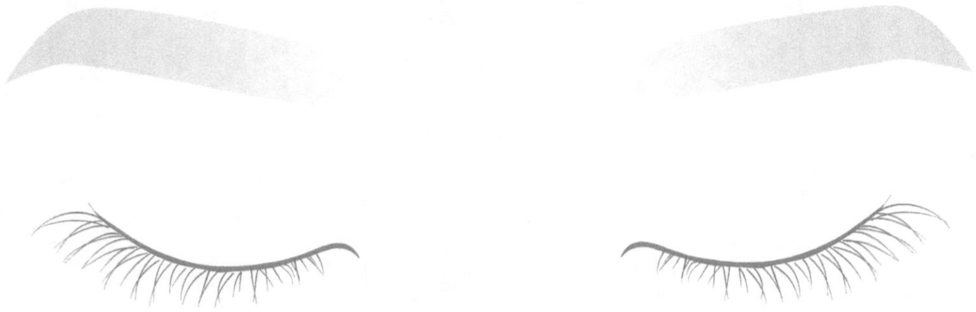

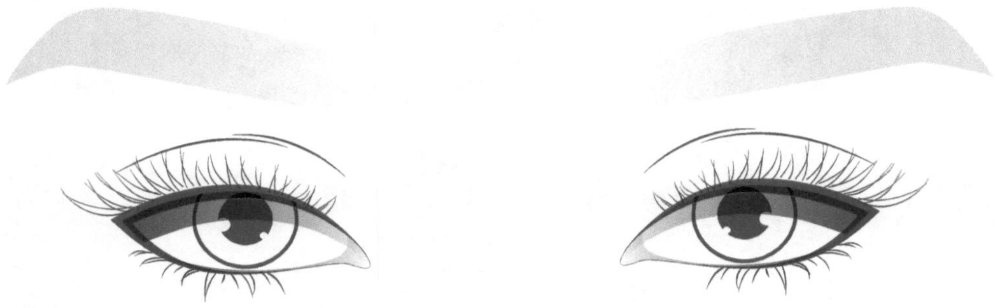

Notes

Try your colors

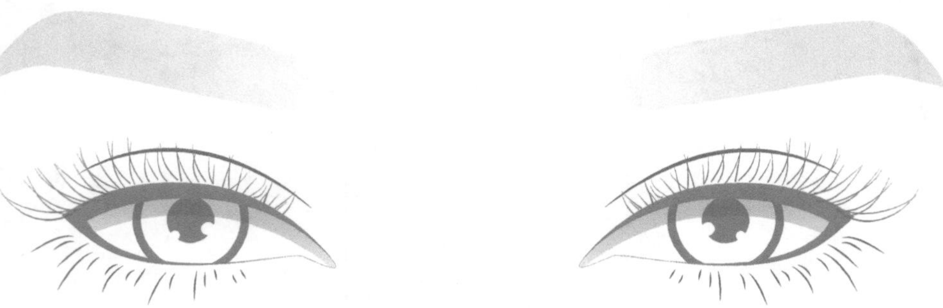

Notes

Try your colors

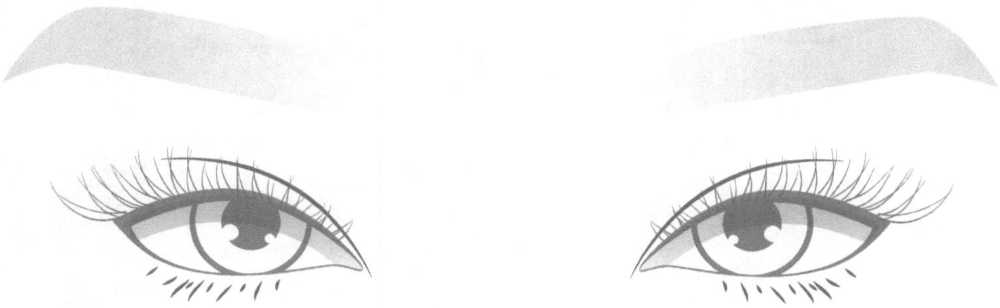

Notes

Try your colors

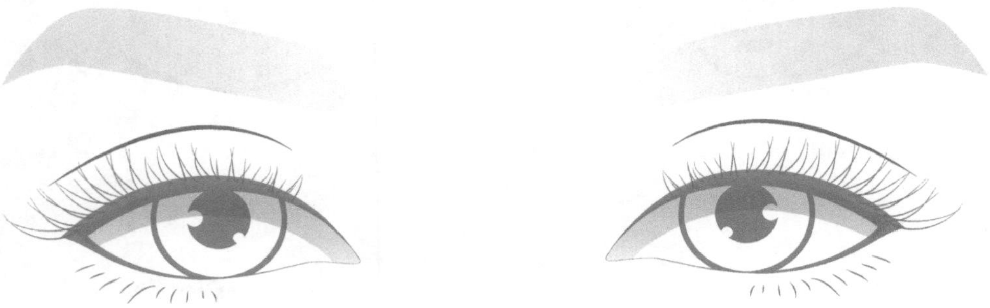

Notes

Try your colors

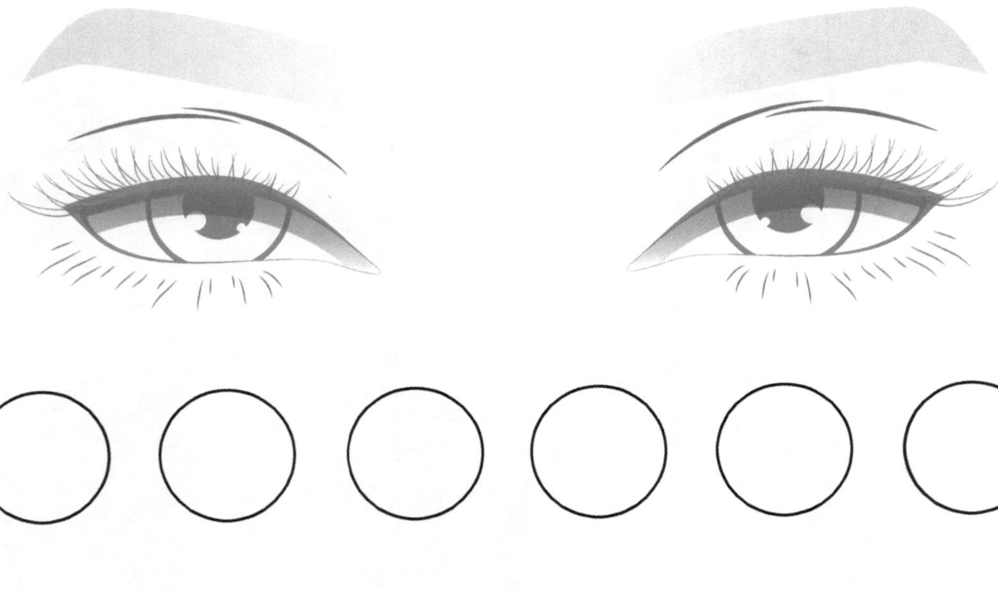

Notes

Notes

Made in United States
Troutdale, OR
11/28/2023

15075509R00113